Dancing With Money

Dancing With Money

Seven Skills To Improve Your Personal Finances

Kayla Tenboer-Sipes

Summer Haven Publishing

CONTENTS

Published by Summer Haven Publishing
Morrison, Illinois
summerhavenpublishing@gmail.com

Editors: Kelvin Tenboer and Sara Tenboer

Front and Back Cover Photographer: Cheeky Gallery

Author Headshot Photographer: Jill Beswick Photography

First Printing, 2024

DEDICATION

I want to thank all of my dance teachers and coaches for pushing me to be the best that I can be. If I wouldn't have learned these dance skills then I wouldn't be the financial rockstar that I am today. So, thank you, for teaching me the skills needed to be a great dancer.

I also want to thank my parents for investing so much money into my dance lessons and the priceless dance trips that I experienced. Also, for all the times you came to watch me perform.

Thank you to my teammates and fellow dancers for all the fun times we danced together.

Thank you, Jennifer Alvarado, for teaching me that you don't have to receive the first-place trophy to be number one in your own heart. You become number one by putting in the hard work, not by the results of the competition.

As I sit on my parent's back steps, the cold draft turns my toes into icicles. I sniffle with every sharp breath. The green floral carpet pokes me through my tan tights causing my skin to itch. The tears start to freeze as they go down my face.

"I'm not going to dance tonight!" I yell to my mom.

"Kayla, if you don't go to dance tonight, then we are telling your dance teacher that you are done for the year," my mom replies.

"Fine!," I stomp my feet as I go back into the house and start taking off my leotard.

I was five years old, I had thoughts in my mind but didn't know how to express them to others. I had a deep desire not to go to dance that night. Why? For one simple reason, which I was too embarrassed to admit. Instead of telling my mom the truth, I threw a fit. Does anyone else have a child like that?

The truth about that night was that I was embarrassed to do "London Bridge is Falling Down," in front of all the parents. Instead of telling my mom and teacher that I didn't want to participate in this "fun" activity, I avoided the situation altogether. And that, my friend, is how many people react to adult responsibilities like their finances.

People would rather avoid the topic of finances instead of facing them head-on. They would rather go through life ignoring the truth of how finances work. They hide under the covers and hope everything will work out. They would rather take the easiest route that results in short-term peace of mind, instead of pushing themselves to learn new skills so they have long-term financial freedom.

With the right skills and mindset, finances can bring meaning and purpose to our lives. To accomplish this, we have to be brave enough to face the truth about our financial situation and be motivated enough to create new habits that cause financial progress. To move our mindset in the right direction we can compare finances to something more fun and relatable. Something that most people recognize as a universal language. Dance!

To be a good dancer we have to acquire many skills. The same is true for finances. In fact: dance and finances share many of the same skills and that is what we will be going over in this quick read book. By understanding these skills we can come out from under the covers and face the "scary monster" called finances. We will be able to implement these body and mind skills to our everyday lives, so we can discover hope in our finances.

The seven skills we will cover are as follows:

1. Control
2. Focus
3. Balance
4. Flexibility
5. Habits
6. Consistency
7. Trust

Five years after the "London Bridge" avoidance, my friend, Erica, asked me to join her dance class at the other studio in town. I agreed to participate in this new terrifying experience. Questions ran through my mind as my dad drove me to my first class:

"Do they do London Bridge at this studio, too?"

"Are they going to require me to do it in front of the parents?"

"I'm older now, so there is no way they will make me do London Bridge...right?"

Those fears disappeared five minutes into class when I realized I had a bigger obstacle to face. Because I was scared to speak my mind and face my fears when I was five, the other girls were all ahead of me with their dance skills. I had wasted five years of practicing dance. Now, I was behind and would have to catch up by working harder. The girls around me had perfect control over their bodies as they did an arabesque. They were able to spot during a perfect pirouette turn. They were balancing on relevé while I was falling toward the barre. They were able to kick above their shoulders, while I could only kick waist high. They had learned their bad habits of sickling their toes and now had perfect pointed feet. They had the ability and stamina to practice over and over without a break and no mistakes. Lastly, I didn't trust in my skills or have the same bond that the other girls had formed. My five minutes of weakness and childish behavior had set me behind and I would have to work quadruple the hours to catch up to my classmate's abilities.

I ended up participating in both dance studios in town and was on the high school dance team. I took ballet, tap, and jazz at one studio, and clogging, modern, and contemporary at the other studio. The dance team practiced five days a week working on our jazz, pom, and kick routines. This hard work resulted in us winning state three out of the four years I was on the team.

I participated in the Macy's Day Parade in 2011. I trained with Mandy Moore from "So You Think You Can Dance," at the Orange Bowl and Holiday Bowl in 2012 and 2013, respectively. I was stretching every time I watched TV, doing tendus while waiting in the lunch line, and doing leaps down the high school hallways. With all of these hours of catch-up, I finally did it. I got to the same level of skill as my classmates.

This same thing can happen with our finances. The longer we avoid our finances, the more work we will have to do to catch up to reach our goals. The more time you waste, the more time you are losing out on compound interest working for you in your retirement accounts. Now is the time to come out from under the covers and start working toward your financial goals. Today is the day that you decide to view finances as a fun dance toward success. Let's take the first leap together as we learn how to take control of our finances. Ready...5, 6, 7, 8...

Skill 1: Control

Dance:

If you want to look like a professional dancer on stage, then you must have control of your body. You have to know **what** dance move to perform, **where** to perform it on stage and **when** to do the move. If a dancer is not in control, the audience will be able to tell by the mistakes they make with their movements and the scared look in their eyes.

In contrast, when a dancer has control over their body, confidence shines through to the audience, which results in a successful performance.

Finances:

Controlling The 3 W's (What, Where, When)

To have control of our personal finances we have to know what we want to do with our money, where it is going, and when it will be used. The first thing we have to do is decide **what** we will do with our money. The three things you can do with your income are give, save, or spend. Then, we have to decide **where** the money will go. We do this by creating a budget with the EveryDollar app. By creating your budget you are telling every dollar what its job is for the month. Finally, we have to control **when** the money will flow in and out of your bank account. We do this by creating a cash flow plan. We use this plan to make sure the money is going where it's supposed to go at the right time so by the end of the month we have completed a flawless money dance.

What To Do With Our Income

Income:

Start your budget by reviewing your last six paychecks. This information will tell you what type of income you have: fixed or irregular. If you have a **fixed** income then put the total amount you receive in one month as your income at the top of the budget. If you have an **irregular** income, then budget with the lowest amount you can possibly make in a month. We do this for two reasons:

1. If you budget for more than you make, then you won't have enough money to make it through the month, you will get discouraged and want to stop budgeting.
2. If you budget less and get paid more, then you will be excited and have extra money to throw toward your goal. This excitement will motivate you to keep budgeting.

Now that we know how much income we have to deal with, we can start telling our money **what** to do. Everybody will have different percentages based on what season of life they are in, but this is a standard breakdown of what to do with your income.

Give- 10%
Save- 15%
Spend- 75%

Now that we know what we are doing with our income, we will break it down even further by telling it **where** it will go in a written budget.

Telling Your Money Where To Go
Give:

Your giving will be based on your personal preference. I believe that giving allows you to open your heart to gratitude and shows God that you are a good manager of your money and can be trusted with more income. In my personal experience I have seen time and time again that when we give, God gives us the *opportunity* to make more money. This extra work allows us to not only tithe, but also donate to organizations we are passionate about.

Give based on your passions and what your heart is telling you. If you are passionate about your church then give a tithe. If you are an animal lover, then give to your local animal shelter. Discover your passions and research organizations that work within your passions. Your donations can most likely be used as tax deductions, but don't give for that reason. Make sure you are doing it out of the kindness of your heart. Use the EveryDollar app to break down where your giving will go. Specify the organization's name and the amount you are giving.

Think outside the box about additional ways to give to your community with your time and talents. Your could volunteer your time at a homeless shelter to serve meals. As a photographer, you could donate your photography skills to capture precious moments for families that have children with special needs. You could be a good role model to the next generation by becoming a part of the Boys & Girls Club of America. What talents and time can you donate to give back to your community?

Save:

The standard is to save 10% - 20% of your income every month. Once you have paid off all of your debt and have created an emergency fund that covers 3-6 months of expenses, then it is good practice to save 15% of your income into retirement accounts. What percentage you save will be based on the season of life you are in.

Examples of increasing your saving percentage:

- If you are expecting a child, then you will want to save as much as possible to cover your max out-of-pocket for hospital expenses. You will also want to save enough to offset being off work for maternity leave.

- If you know you will have to move soon, then you will want to save up as much as possible to make the move a smooth transition cash flow wise. You will also want to create a large down payment. It is ideal to put 20% down so you don't have to pay PMI (private mortgage insurance).

- If you know your car is getting to the end of its life, then you will want to save up to pay cash for a new car.

- If you know your workplace is having layoffs, and you might be the next one to lose their job, then you will want to save up as much as possible so you have funds to cover your needs while you are looking for a new job.

- If you are within twenty years of retirement and have nothing saved and no pension plan, then you will want to contribute as much as you can toward retirement accounts.

Being proactive and aware of your season of life will prepare you for what is coming. This allows you to be in control and have peace of mind as you go through transitions in life. We will go deeper into where to save your money during Skill 6: Consistency.

Spend:

Use the EveryDollar app to input your four walls. These are the four budget categories that you need to survive through the month. Add up the total of your four walls and write it here. We will reference this page in Skill 6: Consistency. The four walls include:

1. Mortgage/Rent
2. Utilities
3. Food (Groceries only)
4. Transportation

Total:_____

Next, scroll to the bottom of the app to put in your minimum debt payments.

Then, fill in any monthly bills that you consider a "need" in this day in age. (Ex. cell phone and internet)

Lastly, put in any other expenses that you might run into this month. (Ex. wedding, birthday party)

> Tips:
> -Don't forget pet costs
> -Budget at least $100 in a miscellaneous category
> -Create sinking funds for large **expected** expenses
> (Learn more in Skill 6: Consistency)

At the top of the app it will tell you how much money you have left to budget or if you are over budget. If you have money left over then put that amount toward your goal, whether that is saving or paying off debt. Adjust the budget until you have a zero-based budget.

> Notice, I did not have you include fun spending in your budget. These additional categories include: restaurants, fun money, clothing, vacations, hair/cosmetics, etc. Before you put in your "wants" we want to discover how much income you have left over after your needs are met. Knowing this amount is your opportunity cost of adding in your "wants" instead of prioritizing your goal. After we know this amount, then you can add in your "wants" while being mindful of what you are prioritizing.

Telling Your Money When It Will Be Used

Cash Flow Plan

What is cash flow? Cash flow is the movement of your cash going in and out of your bank account. We must create a cash flow plan to make sure that you have money in your bank account throughout the whole month and into the following month until your next paycheck comes in. Without a plan, you can easily overdraw your bank account and get charged an overdraft fee. By doing simple math (adding and subtracting) we can create this plan. The hard part is sticking to the plan based on your budgeted numbers. Here are the steps to take to make sure you will have enough money in your bank account until the middle of the following month.

Step 1: Find a piece of paper and write the current balance of your bank account at the top.

Step 2: Number 1-31 on the left side of your paper.

Step 3: Review your upcoming bills: write -$$$ on the line that correlates with the day that bill will come out of your bank account.

Step 4: Write in your income +$$$ on the line that correlates with the day your paycheck will come through your bank account.

Step 5: Based on the budget we just made in EveryDollar; subtract any variable expenses that you will need throughout the month. (groceries, gas- split them up based on how often you buy them: weekly, biweekly, monthly)

Step 6: Go down the paper and subtract and add what your balance will be each day of the month.

Step 7: Flip over your paper and repeat these steps into the next month by putting your end of month balance as the beginning of month balance on the back. Make sure you will have enough money to cover all of your beginning of month bills before your next paycheck comes in.

If your balance goes below $0 that means you have a slight cash flow issue. We can fix this issue a couple ways.

1. Talk with lenders to adjust what day they will pull your payment.

2. Talk with lenders about paying biweekly so you aren't taking such a large hit in one day.

3. Create a larger buffer in your checking account.

4. Adjust the day you spend money from any of your variable categories. (groceries, fun, gas)

The goal with our cash flow plan is to never go negative in our bank account **and** to find days that we can throw more money toward our goals.

Living on Budget

In 2019, Evan and I hit rock bottom. We received an unexpected hospital bill that we couldn't pay. After realizing that we had messed up financially by spending more than we made, I decided to take finance classes on Coursera.org to learn everything I could about money. Then I created a paper budget and continued living our lives like normal. Two years went by and our personal finances didn't improved. I asked myself, "How can we create a budget and have all this new knowledge about finances and not see any progress?"

That's when I realized that we may have made a budget, but we weren't living on said budget. I might have new knowledge, but I wasn't putting that knowledge into action. That's when I learned that knowledge + action = progress. If we want to make progress with our finances then we have to put in the work to create new habits that promote progress.

To start seeing progress we have to be in control throughout the whole month by tracking every transaction that we make. To do this successfully, we have to create good habits of immediately inputting the transaction when we make the purchase. It takes a minute or less to input a purchase which is the same amount of time it takes a cashier to finish your transaction. So, start practicing this new habit today when you're checking out at the store.

Create Your Money Dance Choreography

Create your first budget in the EveryDollar app. Decide to take control of your money and live on a budget. Then, create a cash flow plan so your money knows when it will be used.

Giving your income a purpose, gives your job purpose, which gives your life purpose!

2

Skill 2: Focus

Dance:

When completing a successful turn in dance, we have to focus on a single spot in the direction we want to go. You wouldn't use a wall as your spot because it's too large of an area. Instead, you should use a stationary small point like a sticker on the wall.

Focusing on this single point will keep you moving in the right direction. As your body moves in a circular motion your eyes and head will whip around faster than your body to continue focusing on the spot. This head movement gives your body additional momentum to complete the desired turn.

If you lose focus on your spot, your body will follow your eyes wherever it is looking. This often will cause you to lose balance and fall to one side. This will result in you not completing your turn successfully and not being able to perform the next movement correctly or on time.

Finances:

In finances we have to have that same focus but instead of focusing on your "spot," we are focusing on a goal. To stay in control of your budget you want to keep your desired goal in mind. To create your goal you should specify your POWERS.

P- Purpose
O- Outlook
W- Written
E- Exact
R- Reward
S- Support

P- Purpose

Understanding the purpose for wanting to reach your goal gives you a higher chance of accomplishing said goal. To discover the real purpose behind reaching your goal we ask ourselves "why" three times. Often, your first "why" isn't the real reason, but it's a symptom of a deeper "why." We want to discover the "why" that is festering within. This "why" is the reason you will be motivated to keep going because it usually stems from a past traumatic experience. Those deep feelings within are what will push you to the finish line. I call this your "Iceberg Why" since it is usually the hidden feeling underneath that cause the most damage. Here is an example to get your brain thinking in the right direction:

Goal: Paying Off Our Debt

Why? I want to get rid of our debt so we can start
reaching other financial goals.
Why? I want to be able to travel with my kids and show them
the world without having a credit card bill when we get home.
Why? When I grew up, everyone in school would talk about
their fun summer vacations, but my parents couldn't afford to
take us on vacation, so I felt left out.
I don't want that for my children.

Notice the difference between the first "why" and the last "why?" You went from having a blanket statement that most people relate to and narrowed it down to why that statement relates specifically to you, your life, and your feelings. You discovered the reason why your past is affecting you today. When you discover these feelings it gives your goal more meaning. This will keep you motivated to reach your goal.

Discover Your Iceberg Why:

Goal: _____

Why?_____

_____

Why?_____

_____

Why?_____

_____

O- Outlook

When creating your goal it's important to know the outlook of your life. By looking ahead we become aware of upcoming events that might affect the ability to accomplish your goal. Based on these events we create a timeline. Take in account weddings, vacations, the cost of adding a family member, or anything else that has a large ticket price. Take in account each of these life transitions and add more time to your timeline. Decide on a date that you want to reach your goal. This includes a month, day, and year.

When we don't acknowledge our outlook then we will most likely get derailed by life events that will cost us delays in reaching our goal. This delay will cause us to lose momentum and discourage us from continuing to work toward our goal.

W- Written

Studies have shown that you are 42% more likely to accomplish your goal if it is written down.[1] Write down your goal and keep it front and center in your day-to-day life. Write it on a paper and put it on your bathroom mirror, refrigerator, or front door. That way you see it every day when you leave the house. Put your POWERS statement as the background on your cell phone so you stay motivated throughout the day. Having your goal written out makes your goal a real tangible item in our world instead of a floating thought in your head.

E- Exact

Specifying your exact goal gives you a way of knowing when you have reached your goal. This could be an exact money amount, weight loss goal, or a position at work. Knowing exactly what you are working toward allows your brain to stay focused on one exact "spot." Once you know this amount then you can break it down into milestones and reward yourself along the journey.

R- Reward

To keep you motivated in reaching your goal we can use the psychology behind rewards. Make your reward equivalent to the size of your goal. If you are working on a large goal like paying off $80,000 of consumer debt, then your reward wouldn't be to get yourself a coffee at your favorite coffee shop. Your reward would be much larger like going on a vacation for your great accomplishment. But, to get you to the large reward we can use smaller rewards. Motivate yourself every month with a reward for accomplishing small wins. For example: if you stay within your budget this month, then you get to go to the movies for a date night. This reward releases dopamine and will motivate you to continue the good behaviors of sticking to your budget so you get another reward the next month.[2] Write down the rewards you will give yourself to stay accountable and motivate you to reach your goal.

> Tip:
> Make sure to include your reward cost in your budget.

S- Support

To successfully reach your goal we want to have support from loved ones and friends. Write down who you want to be your support system throughout your POWERS goal journey. Talk with those people and let them know exactly how they can support you. You can ask them to check in on you every week. Have them send you motivational quotes to keep you going. Or be a set of ears to listen when you need to vent or get feedback. Having a support system will keep you headed toward your goal and not get distracted. They will also be another layer of accountability to keep you on track.

POWERS Statement

My goal is to_____
(EXACT GOAL)

_____

by_____because_____
(MM/DD/YYYY))   (THIRD WHY))

_____

_____.

When I reach this goal I will
reward myself with_____
(REWARD)

_____.

My support system includes

_____and
(SUPPORT PERSON)

_____.
(SUPPORT PERSON)

Skill 3: Balance

Dance:

We all know what happens when a dancer loses their balance in the middle of a turn. That's right...they fall. To keep your balance you have to stay focused on your spot and be in control of your body. You must tighten your core muscles and align your hips and shoulders. You have to have strong muscles to keep your balance from head to toe.

While doing ballet, if we feel off balance our gut instinct will be to grab the closest sturdy thing to us, which is usually the barre. By grabbing the barre we can realign our shoulders and hips, find our focus, and regain our balance. But if there is nothing to grab and your hip drops, then your shoulder and head are going to follow and you will go tumbling down.

Finances:

Creating balance in our lives will automatically help us with our finances. You will know you are out of balance when your body is in one place, and your mind is in another. The most popular reference to balance is work-life balance. When you are at work, you are thinking about your kids, and when you are home with your kids, you are responding to work emails.

To regain balance we often try to find something we can take control of which usually results in spending money. We go to the nail salon and get a mani-pedi to feel pretty. We go to the spa to get a massage. We book a vacation, just to "get away from life." This often causes us to go outside our budget and overspend.

To keep our balance we have to protect our priorities, establish boundaries, acknowledge gratitude, and practice patience. By aligning these four areas of our life we create balance, just like when we align our shoulders and hips to successfully complete a turn. If one of the four areas of our life is pulled out of place, then it will pull the other areas out of line as well causing discontentment. Creating this alignment is our balancing act to find contentment and stay true to our values, finances, and goals.

Performing a Balancing Act

Priorities

To protect our priorities we have to acknowledge the season of life we are in and look at the goals we created under our Skill 2: Focus. Knowing these goals will help us create a list of our priorities that we want to protect at this moment in life. Once we have our list of five priorities (most important to least important) we can use this list to help us create our budget.

If your priority is to pay off debt then any remaining funds will go to pay off your lowest debt. If your priority is to save for a house, then extra money will go into a savings account for a down payment. If you want to prioritize self-care, then make a category to go to the spa and relax. Your budget should reflect whatever your priorities are for this month. Once you have that budget created to support those priorities, then it's your job to protect that budget with your boundaries.

Boundaries

Your budget is your financial boundary. All other boundaries that you create are made to protect the priorities in your budget. Creating boundaries puts you in control of your life. You are the one that draws the line in the sand preventing anyone or yourself from going outside of your budget. To keep this protection we have to have self-control.

Money vs. Yourself

Understanding your habits will help you create boundaries to protect yourself from going outside of your budget. If you know that you never leave Target spending less than $150 and having a Venti Praline cold brew in your hand, then create a boundary and drive past Target instead of going in the store. Protect yourself from your own habits so you continue to make progress toward your goals.

Money vs. Relationships

This boundary could be against lending money to a family member or friend when they ask you. By knowing your goals and your budget you can confidently create a boundary and offer to help based on your budget, not your heartstrings. This could mean you find money in the budget to give your friend money instead of lending it to them. Or you could find other ways to help them aside from money. Like cooking them a meal or babysitting for them. By setting boundaries you are creating a clear understanding between both parties which should keep the relationship healthy and strong.

Money vs. Marriage

This last boundary is actually the idea of having a lack of boundary. If you want to make progress with your finances when you are married then you need to get rid of the financial boundaries between you and your spouse. That means it is "our" money, not "his" or "her" money. You must communicate with your spouse to create shared goals and create a plan on how you will reach that goal as a team. That means creating the family budget together. It means being open about your spending habits. It means talking about buying something before purchasing it. Taking down boundaries puts you on the same team so you can create more progress in a shorter time frame.

Gratitude

In November 2023, I went on a last-minute trip to the Netherlands and Denmark for my best friend's wedding. It was a week-long trip of experiencing foreign food, playing frogger across the Netherland streets, attempting not to get hit by a biker, and hunting for unique smoking pipes for our collection. It was an amazing trip that I will never forget. When arriving home safely I jumped in bed to relax and I pulled out the handy dandy Facebook app. As I started to scroll I saw a friend's post that they were in Mexico and all of my exciting adventure jitters disappeared. I started getting jealous of my friend's trip that she got to go on instead of being thankful for the wonderful trip that I just experienced. This feeling pulled me out of balance as I started to feel discontent with my life.

Technology often causes us to compare our lives to others and downgrade our wonderful life to a mediocre one. Jealousy sneaks in and we tend to lose sight of what actually matters, which are the priorities that we listed above. My priority was not to sit on a beach and enjoy Pina Coladas, it was to support my best friend and her marriage. And that's exactly what I accomplished. As these thoughts of successfully acting on my priorities ran through my head I started to smile and I put my phone away. If we don't remind ourselves of our priorities we often start saying, "if only."

"If only I had a bigger house, then I will be happy. If only I had a nicer car, then I will be more successful than my friend. If only I had kids, then my marriage will get better."

All the "if onlys" flooding your head are drowning you in your own tears. To break this cycle, we have to be thankful for what we have. This gratitude will fill us with happiness and restore balance so you can stay true to your priorities and boundaries.

Patience

Without patience in your plan, you will start making mistakes that cause you to go outside your budget. God likes to play funny jokes on me. Every time I ask for patience, He doesn't give it to me, but rather He gives me an opportunity to practice patience. One way to practice patience with finances is to see if the purchase can fit in the budget. If you can't fit it in the budget then it's God's way of saying, "No." This just means that you will have to be patient to buy the item until the cash is there.

"No" is not a negative word, it just means you are saying "yes " to something else. For example: I am saying "yes" to saving for my retirement instead of spending hundreds on going out to eat every month. If your priorities change, then adjust the budget the next month to buy the thing that you had to say "no" to this month. The cool thing is that it's called personal finance. So you can do whatever you want with your budget. The key is to stay in control and be intentional about your budget decisions.

Patience Paying Off Debt

If you are working on paying off debt you will be tempted to throw the lump sum toward your debt right when you receive your paycheck. Although that is great determination, it isn't wise. We must be patient so we have the proper cash flow to make it to your next paycheck. Refer to your cash flow plan from Skill 1: Control, to discover the best times to throw extra money toward your debt.

> Tips:
> If you have $400 allocated toward your debt then I recommend you pay off $100 every week. This will help keep you motivated and it will lower the interest that is due.

Priorities

(WRITE OUT YOUR PRIORITIES FROM
MOST IMPORTANT TO LEAST IMPORTANT)

1._____

2._____

3._____

4._____

5._____

Gratitude

(WRITE OUT FIVE THINGS YOU ARE GRATEFUL FOR)

1._____

2._____

3._____

4._____

5._____

Skill 4: Flexibility

Dance:

When watching a dance team perform, you will notice that one or two individuals will most likely be front and center performing cool acrobatic tricks. This person is most likely the most flexible person on the team. When you are more flexible you get to be in the spotlight more. You get to do fun tricks that others aren't able to do.

Finances:

Being flexible with your finances enables you to accept the changes that happen throughout the month. It gives you the confidence to change the budget without getting discouraged. This proves that you are a problem solver. It shows that you don't panic under pressure, but instead face the problem at hand. This might be an unexpected hospital bill, a car repair, or a last-minute birthday party invite.

When an unexpected cost arises; you will have the knowledge and confidence to adjust the budget and continue in life like nothing happened. The first thing you will want to do is assess your current budget. Then, add in the new budget category with the amount that you have to spend. Once you know how much you are over budget, we will start deducting small amounts from each variable budget category. This could be $5-$20 from several different categories. These are the categories that aren't bills, meaning they are 100% controlled by you and your spending habits. This will help you find money without "shocking" a single category. By doing this, you won't feel the strain as much as if you pulled it all from one category.

If you have reduced all of the categories that you can and you are still over budget, then you will have to pull funds from savings to cover the difference. If you don't have money saved, then it's time to get creative and look for opportunities to increase your income.

Your best return of your time would be working overtime at your full-time job. If your job doesn't offer overtime, then I encourage you to write down your talents and find a side gig that aligns with your skills and passions. For example: if you love kids then offer babysitting on your days off. If you love baking then see if a local bakery is hiring for the early shift that you can go in before your full-time job. If you are crafty then sell your beautiful creations at craft fairs or on Etsy. The sky's the limit if you put in the time and effort to discover what you love and look for opportunities to increase income.

By putting in the hard work to increase your income instead of grabbing the credit card to save you; you build self-accomplishment and confidence. Trusting in yourself and your abilities helps you become a better version of yourself.

Being flexible gives you the confidence to be center stage while you stick to a goal oriented budget.

5

Skill 5: Habits

Dance:

Every dancer has habits that have to be broken so they look like all the other dancers. To discover these habits, dance instructors will videotape the movement or performance and watch it in slow motion to see what habits need to change or be broken. These are often little things like hunching when doing a kick, not pointing your toes when leaping, or rotating your hips during a turn. By examining the footage we can point out these bad habits and alter them to improve their dance skills.

Finances:

Discovering your spending habits is an important part of successfully living on a budget and reaching your goals. You can discover these habits in two ways: evaluating past transactions and realizing your emotional spending habits.

Evaluating Past Transactions

To discover our habits, we do the highlighter exercise.

1. Print out three months of bank statements.

2. Grab 5-10 different colored highlighters, colored pencils, or crayons.
3. Create a key in the top corner of your statement. Each color will represent a different budget category.
4. Go through each statement, highlighting what category each transaction goes in.
5. Add up each month's categories.
6. Calculate the average of each category based on the totals for those three months.
7. Reflect on how much you spent in each category. Did your jaw just drop?

Now that we know how much you were spending in each category of your budget, we can see where your habits lie. Find what category you spent the most in. Why did you spend that much? Was it normal to spend that much, or did you have a special occasion that caused that category to be so high? Maybe you had two weddings to attend, so you had to spend more than normal on hotels, eating out, and gas. Use this information to plan better for future events by creating sinking funds.

Look at categories that you should cut back on. Did you spend too much on fun things? Did you overspend on groceries? Maybe you drove more than normal, and you could have saved on gas if you went shopping at closer stores. Maybe you got coffee every day from your favorite barista and never realized how much it was *really* costing you. That $7 coffee five days a week costs you $140 a month and $1,680 a year. What else could you have done with that $1,680? Reflect on your habits and make decisions to reduce certain categories so you can prioritize more money to reach your goal.

If you are overspending in certain categories, they most likely will be fun categories that you use a debit or credit card to purchase. Consider purchasing a cash envelope wallet to help create self-control. At the start of the month, you can put the budgeted amount of cash in each of your envelopes. Use this wallet as a tool to teach you not to overspend. Once the cash is gone from your envelope, then you physically can't spend more. This is teaching you good habits on how to stick to your budget.

Tip:
If you can't afford to fill all of your envelopes at the start of the month then divide them based on your paycheck and refill them weekly or biweekly.

Another important part of the highlighting exercise is to make sure that you don't have any fraudulent activity in your account or have subscriptions that you didn't realize you were paying for. Many people find at least one subscription that they didn't know they had. This is an easy way to save money because you don't use that service anyway.

Habits can be difficult to alter, especially if you aren't clear on what the reward is for changing those habits. Start changing those habits just by being aware of when you are doing them. Point them out to yourself. When you grab your keys and leave early for work so you can stop at your favorite coffee shop, pause, and remind yourself what your end goal is. Instead of paying $7 for your morning coffee, you decide to make a cappuccino at home. Boom! Seven dollars more to throw at your goal!

Acknowledge Your Habits

Habit 1:_____

_____

Habit 2:_____

_____

Habit 3:_____

_____

My Spending Habit

In March of 2020, it was a typical day working at Redeemed Office in DeKalb, Illinois. I was creating office layouts on AutoCAD, updating the inventory on their website, and attempting to think of creative content for social media when I received a text from my cousin that said, "I love you. Stay strong. Let me know if you need anything." My eyebrows furrowed, my lips pursed. My head slightly tilted as my eyes wandered up, looking for an answer. "Maybe she sent the text to the wrong person?" I called my mom to see if she knew what my cousin was talking about.

My parents just found out that my dad was diagnosed with kidney cancer. My world flipped upside down. I couldn't think straight. I couldn't work efficiently, and I couldn't drive the hour and a half back home. I talked to my boss and she drove me home to be with my family. The next day, I was still in panic mode. I shopped and shopped and shopped until I dropped. I spent $1,000 that day, and I didn't care because all my emotions and thoughts were on my dad and his cancer. Regret snuck in three days later when I realized how much I had spent. Talk about buyer's remorse. Too bad I had already used everything so nothing could be returned.

Weeks later, they took out his kidney, and he was cancer-free. Praise the Lord.

Three years go by and my dad had his annual checkup. My mom called me when I was rushing home to get the baby formula I had forgotten. My mother was crying. I asked her what was wrong. "Did you get my text yesterday," she asked. "No," I replied. She continued to inform me that Dad's scans came back, and there was a spot on his lung. There was a 95% chance it was cancer, and we were told he had five years to live.

This time around, I knew my habits. I knew what these intense emotions going through my body were wanting me to do. I needed to shop....now! But this time instead of going on a shopping spree,

I paused and looked at my budget. I figured out how much I could spend without going over budget that month. I was able to find $100 to spend. By the end of the shopping spree, I spent $93. This time, I was in control of my emotions and my budget instead of my emotions controlling me. Because I knew my habits, I was able to control them and the situation I was in. So that way, after going shopping, I was proud of myself instead of feeling ashamed. I acknowledged my habits and changed them so it worked for me, instead of against me.

I encourage you to reflect on past emotions and shopping sprees to find any correlations. By knowing the que that caused us to act out our bad habits, we can create better new habits that help us stay on budget.

Habit Changes

When_____
(QUE)

Instead of:_____
(HABIT 1)

I will:_____
(NEW HABIT)

_____.

◆──◆

When_____
(QUE)

Instead of:_____
(HABIT 2)

I will:_____
(NEW HABIT)

_____.

◆──◆

When_____
(QUE)

Instead of:_____
(HABIT 3)

I will:_____
(NEW HABIT)

6

Skill 6: Consistency

Dance:

Any dance routine you watch I can assure you that the team has practiced countless hours to accomplish the performance that you witnessed. They have rehearsed the routine over and over. They have drilled every kick, pom move, and turn like it's the last thing they will do. This repetition will create consistency of performing the proper movement out of habit. This will ensure that when recital day comes our fears of being on stage won't stop us from doing the right moves. This consistency leads to a confident successful performance.

Finances:

If you want to experience progress and a sense of accomplishment with your finances then you have to be willing to put in the hard work to create a habit of consistently saving money month after month. This means part of your budget will be prioritizing your future self. There are three types of savings and each one of them has a different amount, purpose, and timeline of being used. These three savings are your emergency fund, personal savings, and retirement savings. Your future self will thank you for the sacrifices you are making today when saving part of your income.

Emergency Fund

The emergency fund is your three to six months of bare minimum expenses that will cover an emergency like a job loss. Save this money in a high-yield savings account connected to your checking account, where it can be transferred within days.

First, you will want to decide how many months of expenses you need saved to satisfy your security gland. Then, refer to page 5 where you calculated the cost of your four walls (mortgage/rent, utilities, food, and transportation) and multiply that amount by how many months you want to have saved. Save up this much as fast as possible so you feel secure in life.

We aren't looking to make money off this savings; we are looking to use it as our first form of defense against unexpected expenses. But, at the same time, shop around to find the best money market with the highest interest rate. This might mean you will put it in an online savings account. This money is used for **unexpected** expenses only. In addition, this emergency fund gives you the financial freedom to change directions in your career if your job isn't fulfilling your purpose in life. Before using your emergency fund think of NUN and ask yourself these three questions:

N: Needed? - Is this purchases **needed** in my life? Or is it a want?
U: Unexpected? - Is this purchase **unexpected**?
N: Now? - Does this purchases have to be made right **now**?

If you answer "Yes," to all three of these questions then the expense is a viable reason to use your emergency fund. If you answer "No," to any of the questions, then evaluate what the opportunity cost would be for using the fund for this purchase and how long it will take you to rebuild the fund. If you are okay with these realizations then use the emergency fund for the purchase and rebuild the fund as fast as possible.

Personal Savings

Your personal savings are for things that you plan on buying. This includes any sinking fund you are budgeting for every month. This type of savings should be put in a savings account at your bank that is connected to your checking. These savings should be able to transfer funds instantly. This account usually has a very low-interest rate, less than one percent. This money is used for **expected** expenses. Once you reach your savings goal, then use that money and experience the reward for all the hard work you put into saving for the large purchase. The most rewarding experience I have had is paying cash for two vehicles. Driving off a car dealer's parking lot when you have paid cash for a car has a different feeling. It's magical. Otherwise known as: **freedom**.

Sinking Funds

Murphy's law means that if something can go wrong in life, then it will. Murphy isn't a fun friend to have around, but let's be honest, Murphy always comes around to check in on us. Knowing that something will go wrong is part of life and we want to be prepared when Murphy comes knocking. That's why we use sinking funds to cover these costs. Your car will have problems at one point or another. Your furnace is going to break one of these days. Your refrigerator is going to stop running. And your toilet might overflow and leave you with a flooded house.

Any expense that you can't cash flow in one month should be turned into a sinking fund. This could include any bills that you pay annually. For example: car insurance, life insurance, property taxes, or house insurance. The most common sinking funds include vacations, new furniture or technology, a new car, and Christmas expenses. To calculate your sinking fund you will determine how much total you want to save and then divide that amount by how many months you have to save. This will be the total amount you want to transfer to your personal savings at the end of the month. We use sinking funds as Murphy repellent to protect us, not only financially, but emotionally.

* * *

It was January in the Midwest and we all know that means higher gas bills, snow, and icicles. The temperature in the house was going down as I was turning the heater up. Something wasn't right and that was confirmed when a squealing noise started coming out of the furnace vent. It was a Saturday night and it was time to bundle up with the hubby and get cozy in front of the fireplace in our bedroom until we could call the furnace guy the next morning. Of course, being a Sunday it was considered a "weekend emergency call." So there were extra fees added to our charges.

A piece of paper. That's it. A paper got stuck in the vent and was causing weird noises. At least that's what the company told us. Until the next Saturday when the furnace stopped working again and here comes another "weekend emergency call" fee. Finally, the problem was fixed. After a hefty bill, we had heat. During this whole time, I was frustrated. But I wasn't panicking about having to pay a large bill to have heat in my house. We had created a sinking fund to cover these types of expenses. We were able to pay the bill with cash and move on in life without affecting our current budget. I got my heat fixed and I got extra cuddle time with my husband. How can I complain about that?

Retirement Savings

Retirement savings are used for...you called it...retirement. So, we won't be able to touch it until we are fifty-nine and a half, but time is on our side. We want to start investing as early as we can. Time, diversity, and consistency are key to creating a successful retirement account. The sooner you reach your debt and savings goals, the sooner you can take advantage of compound interest. Investing 15% of your gross income into diverse, long-track record mutual funds is the goal. I recommend you hire a financial advisor with the heart of a teacher to help you make wise decisions with your retirement accounts.

Consistency shows that you are in control as you create good saving habits while reaching your goals.

7

Skill 7: Trust

Dance:

When dancing with a partner or a team, you have to trust in your fellow dancers that they will be where they are supposed to be at the right time. If you are performing lifts then you *really* have to trust your partner to have the strength not to drop you. You must be one with your partner and make sure you have the correct timing with the music so your movement flows into a single flawless dance move. This trust will form with practice and by sharing a goal of wanting the best performance possible.

Finances:

I was a pawn to the credit card company's game. I was obsessed with having a high credit score. I played the credit card shuffle trying to get the most cash back, points, and miles possible. I was playing by the credit card company's terms instead of my terms. I gave my life value based on my credit score. When I got rid of my credit cards I learned that I was playing the wrong game of life. Instead of putting trust in credit card companies, I needed to trust in my abilities to have financial control. I needed to trust that God will take care of my every need. When we decided to say, "Bye Felicia," to the credit card world I learned three important life lessons.

1. A safety net that you create is stronger than any credit card safety net.
2. An intrinsic reward will beat an extrinsic reward any day.
3. When you take the harder path it makes you stronger.

Lesson 1: Creating Your Safety Net

When people say they can't get rid of credit cards because they need it for emergencies, that tells me that they don't have an emergency fund. This means they are putting their trust in a piece of plastic to save them instead of their saving account. It means that they prioritize spending over saving when they created their budget.

Using a credit card as your safety net has no hard work attached to it, so you are more willing to spend the money without a second thought. Your view of another line of credit might protect you in the moment but the instant you don't respect this line of credit and forget to pay the bill you get hit with interest and the safety unravels beneath you and you fall harder than before.

When you take control of your finances and prioritize consistently saving every month, you are proving to yourself that you have self-control and can accomplish any goal you set your mind to. This safety net that you have created proves that you are strong, willing, and able to make progress toward success. You will have more appreciation toward your emergency fund because you have put the hard work and sacrifice into saving the funds. This gives you more respect toward your money which gives it more value than the line of credit you get from your credit card. Your emergency fund is a strongly woven net that protects you and your family from life and provides you interest instead of charging you interest. This will provide you with additional safety net funds when emergencies head your way.

Lesson 2: Intrinsic vs. Extrinsic Rewards

Credit card rewards were a motivating factor for me when I had credit cards. The psychology the credit card companies use for rewards worked on me, which means they are probably working on you as well. In a study done by Dun & Bradstreet they found that on average people spend 12-18% more with a credit card than with cash. Unless a credit card company offers 18% cash back I would say that is not a reward to you. Credit card companies spend more than you will spend in your lifetime to figure out how to entice people with rewards. When we play into the hands of the credit card company we are giving them control of our lives.[3]

Instead of playing by the credit card companies' rules, we can establish a more fulfilling life by creating intrinsic rewards, by taking control of your finances. By honoring your self-worth, your talents, and your passions, you find motivation that you have never experienced before. These characteristics help you become the best version of yourself. When you don't have credit cards allowing you to take shortcuts, you create the life God has planned for you. You can reach goals for your future that you never imagined were possible. You become the hardest-working, most determined, self-motivated person you know because you proved to yourself that you have the power to control your finances. These intrinsic rewards are worth substantially more than any cashback a company offers you.

Lesson 3: Becoming a Stronger Person

When we have the option to use a credit card or work hard to create and stick to a budget, then we will always take the easier option. It is human nature for us to save as much energy as possible to survive, so if there is a shortcut, then we will most likely take it. But, by taking the shortcut we are losing out on becoming a better person.

I believe this little piece of plastic in your wallet called a credit card has changed our mindset and work ethic.

Not having a Credit Card

> "I TOOK THE ONE LESS TRAVELED BY, AND THAT
> HAS MADE ALL THE DIFFERENCE."
> -ROBERT FROST

When you don't have a credit card, it changes your work ethic. When you take away your credit card "safety net," you have to do everything you can to support your family and create a safety net for them. When you don't have a credit card, your only option is to live on a budget and spend less than you make. It requires you to save money. You have no other choice. Your survival instinct will kick in, and you will become a harder worker. You will become more determined to stick to a budget. You will become more motivated to go to work because your job has a purpose: to provide for your family.

Not having a credit card also teaches self-control, communication, decision-making skills, and contentment. When you have to stick to a budget, you learn to say "no" to certain things. It makes you think before you make a purchase. Do you need or want this? It makes you look at your life in a different way. You realize that you have everything you need, because God has provided it for you. These important characteristics will shine through in other parts of your life as well. Your relationship with your spouse, family, and friends will most likely improve because you are prioritizing the things you value in life.

Trusting in yourself creates more rewards than what any plastic card can offer you.

8

Conclusion

Twenty-five years ago I sat on my parent's back steps pouting because I didn't know how to express my feelings and speak my mind. But today, I sit here writing this book to teach the world that finances don't have to be scary like "London Bridge." We can decide today to take the courageous step toward facing our finances. We don't want to lose any more valuable time that we could be using to reach our goals. Whether we have never made a budget, been dealt a bad hand, or stepped into a bad financial mess; you can face the struggles with confidence by applying your seven dance skills to your finances.

Control- When we decide to take control of our finances by budgeting we are setting a precedence to our surroundings that we know what we are doing and when to do it.

Focus- When we focus on creating goals, we prove to the world that we can concentrate on one spot and complete a beautiful turn.

Balance- By aligning our priorities, boundaries, gratitude, and patience we find perfect balance in our day-to-day life.

Flexibility- By becoming more flexible with our budget we discover confidence.

Habits- We learn the truth about our habits whether good or bad and align them with our goals.

Consistency- Applying these skills consistently day in and day out allows us to reach our goals faster.

Trust- And lastly, we find trust in ourselves and in God to help us through the month instead of relying on a credit card.

I lost five years of valuable time that could have been spent improving my dance skills, but more importantly, I lost out on 16 years that I should have paid attention to my finances. On January 2, 2021, my husband, Evan, and I decided to take control of our finances and we cut up ten credit cards. We started to practice these seven dance skills with our finances and were able to pay off $26,000 of debt in four and a half months. Then, we saved up $20,000 in the following six months, which allowed us to pay cash for a van and all of the hospital bills for our twins' births. We accomplished this great feat by working overtime and finding side jobs as we lived on a budget that focused on our priorities. If we can do it, so can you!

When you realize that finances are just little skills that a ten-year-old girl can do, it takes the pressure off your shoulders. It helps you realize that finances don't have to be hard. It just has to be intentional for you to want to improve your life. You don't have to be the best dancer on the stage, but you do want to end the routine knowing that you did your best. By applying these seven dance skills to your financial routine you leave the stage feeling confident in your performance. Get ready as you implement these new skills into your life. 5, 6, 7, 8...You got this!

KAYLA TENBOER-SIPES

Arabesque- Balancing on one foot while extending other leg behind you

Barre- Long skinny bar, parallel to the ground, that dancers hold while performing ballet exercises

Hunching- Rolling shoulders forward causing weak posture (often done during a high kick)

Leaps- Jumping off the ground while extending both of your legs in different positions based on choreographed dance

Pirouette- Turn performed while balancing on relevé while other leg is bent and foot is pointed to knee

Pom- Fluffy ball of material usually cut into small strips with a hidden handle

Relevé- Balancing on one's toes

Sickling- Turning in ones toes instead of being straight from the angle

Spot- Small focal point in front of dancer used to keep balance and momentum

Tendu- Sliding foot along the ground, rolling foot off the ground resulting in a pointed foot

REFERENCES

1. Akgul, B. (2023, March 16). *The Power of Writing Down Goals: 42% More Likely to Achieve Success*. LinkedIn. Retrieved January 11, 2024, from https://www.linkedin.com/pulse/power-writing-down-goals-42-more-likely-achieve-success-banu-akgul

2. Gunn, N. (2023, February 14). *Why Do Incentives Work? The Psychology of Motivation & Rewards*. Extu. Retrieved January 11, 2024, from https://extu.com/blog/incentives-work-psychology-motivation-rewards/

3. Hurd, E., & Konsko, L. (2023, May 31). *Does Using a Credit Card Make You Spend More Money?* Nerdwallet. Retrieved January 11, 2024, from https://www.nerdwallet.com/article/credit-cards/credit-cards-make-you-spend-more

Kayla Tenboer-Sipes is a four-time State Champion in dance and the author of *Dancing with Money: Seven Skills To Improve Your Personal Finances*. As a financial coach, Kayla has morphed her proficient dance skills into financial habits that can be mindlessly incorporated into her clients' lives. Aside from baking her famous chocolate chip cookies in her "dancing kitchen," Kayla enjoys vacationing with her twins, two dogs, and husband at her family's cabin in Hayward, Wisconsin. Kayla's goal is to teach the world that anyone can reach their financial goals by practicing these seven dance skills. If a ten-year-old dancer can do it, so can you!

Follow Me!
Facebook: Kayla Tenboer-Sipes

Contact Me!
kaylatenboersipes@gmail.com